For You

FORGIVE THE BULLY
FOLLOW YOUR BLISS

Design by Austin Partridge
Edited by Cynthia MacDonald
Author Photo Elaheh Mihar

Lightbulb courtesy of OpenClipArt.org

Published by under the imprint Creative Culture

Library and Archives Canada Cataloguing
in Publication

Delorie, Oliver Luke, 1975-, author
        Dear Leroy : forgive the bully & follow your bliss / Oliver Luke Delorie.

ISBN 978-0-9948468-6-0

1. Bullying--Juvenile literature.  2. Self-esteem--Juvenile literature.
I. Title.

BF637.B85D45 2013                    j302.34'3
C2013-907477-5

# TABLE OF CONTENTS


DEAR LEROY ........................................................ 9

FEAR ................................................................ 11

HATERS ............................................................ 13

FORGIVENESS .................................................... 15

ONE IN 7 BILLION ............................................... 17

FAILURE ........................................................... 19

ZOMBIES .......................................................... 21

HAPPINESS ....................................................... 23

PATTERNS ........................................................ 25

OPPOSITES ....................................................... 27

RESPECT .......................................................... 29

CREATIVITY ...................................................... 31

START A BUSINESS ............................................. 33

VOLUNTEER ..................................................... 35

DRUGS ............................................................ 37

ALCOHOL ...................................................... 39

STRESS ........................................................ 41

GO FOR IT .................................................... 43

CRAZY LITTLE ANIMALS ............................. 45

10,000 HOURS ............................................. 47

NO RULES ................................................... 49

MENTORS ................................................... 51

HIGH SCHOOL ........................................... 53

THOUGHTS ARE THINGS ............................ 55

MINDFULNESS .......................................... 57

FOOD IS FUEL ........................................... 59

TIME .......................................................... 61

WORRY ....................................................... 63

PARENTS .................................................... 65

FRIENDS .................................................... 67

SPIRITUALITY ............................................ 69

EVERYTHING IS TEMPORARY ...................... 71

TRAVEL .................................................. 73

POPULARITY ........................................ 75

MONEY ................................................ 77

FINANCIAL FREEDOM ......................... 79

RADICAL ACCEPTANCE ...................... 81

EXERCISE ............................................. 83

BABY STEPS ......................................... 85

YOUR PURPOSE .................................. 87

ROTTEN APPLES ................................. 89

COLLEGE .............................................. 91

LOVE .................................................... 93

TRUST YOURSELF ............................... 95

INSPIRATION ....................................... 96

You are
sunshine.

## DEAR LEROY

I nearly committed bullycide because I thought no one loved me. I actually believed what the bullies said.

They made me question what I looked like; my hairstyle, my teeth, my clothes, my height, my weight, how I walked, how I talked, how I kicked a soccer ball, and how (in their opinion) unattractive to girls I was.

They made fun of my accent, my family, my house, my backpack, my drawings in art class, what I ate for lunch, where I sat, and my shoes.

It was hell and I thought it would never end.

I hope you are smarter than I am, and will do whatever it takes to stop getting pushed around and pressured by your friends to get into trouble, do drugs, drop out of school, or bully other kids.

Why listen to me? Because I was just like you.

I felt like sunshine, and bullies seemed like clouds that liked nothing more than to keep the sun off my face and my world cold and dark and gray, just how they seemed to like it.

But like me, you have something to share with the world, and it's up to you to find out what it is (and learn how to share it) so you can be free.

Fear is only
real if you
believe
in it.

# FEAR

What do you do when you're scared?

Fear is a feeling that was programmed into us humans over thousands of years when we had to hunt and fight saber-toothed tigers (it's not going to go away).

So if fear is only a feeling (like sadness or happiness) it will always come and go.

If you are ever feeling scared, it's okay to run away or to fight, but your feeling of fear is not the enemy.

Don't be angry with yourself. Try not to be mean to your precious little yourself.

Most people fear fear. They are scared of feeling scared.

The sad thing is, this feeling stops them from doing the things they love to do. A feeling!

People are afraid of looking stupid, but who cares? You can always make fun of fear by laughing at it (doing this can turn bullies turn buddies, fyi).

If you are scared of someone or something, they are sucking your power away like a vampire... eek!

Remember: vampires hate sunshine.

Getting bullied
is a good sign.
It means you
are different.

## HATERS

What do you hate?

Hate poisons your heart.

It will quickly kill you, your friends, your family and your dreams.

But only if you let it.

I want you to live. I want to see you grow up big and strong and successful and happy. Don't you?

Hating the people who seem to hate you will only make you weak and sick (even if you are healthy).

When people hate someone or something, they are really hating themselves, but blaming everyone else for how awful they feel.

It doesn't make sense, does it?

I don't believe it's possible for anyone to really hate you... because they don't even know you. They may think they do, but they don't.

It's hard, but hating people will make you sick, sad and lonely. But most importantly, the sun doesn't hate anyone.

How will you get the poison out?

Hate is a poison
that will kill
you slowly.

# FORGIVENESS

Has anyone ever asked you to forgive them?

What did you do or say?

The only reason bullies aren't buddies is because they don't like how much alike you are.

They would never admit this, of course.

I know it seems crazy, but it's true. Years after I graduated, a former bully invited me over to his house to play music with him!

I have also dreamed of bullies asking ME for forgiveness. It was unreal.

I know they didn't mean to hurt me, and I know they don't mean to hurt you. They are rained on by other clouds. It's not their fault.

Of course, you are not a saint. You hurt people. You say and do things you wish you hadn't said or done. But we all do. We are all clouds once-in-a-while.

The secret is to know it. Then do something about it.

But don't beat yourself (or the bullies) up because it's hard for you (and them) to change. Be patient and you will see the miraculous benefit in forgiveness.

It is never
too late to
start again.

# ONE IN 7 BILLION

What makes you unique?

First of all, as the sun, you create high-pressure systems. There is no one on earth quite like you.

Just because you aren't good at something, doesn't mean you aren't good at something else.

I like to say there are 7 billion ways to do everything, and so I believe everyone is free to do things how they want (if they want).

You are probably good at something, and could probably do it all day, every day, right?

Don't let anyone dissuade you or discourage you from making your ideas or plans into something real.

If you're good at sports, play sports. If you're good at music, play music. If you're good at math... do math!

If you ever get worried or scared, and don't know what to do, remember what you like, and do that.

No one knows what you like as much as you do.

And most importantly: let other people do things how they want to do them. If you don't want to be criticized or bossed around, try not to criticize or boss other people around.

Forgiveness
will heal all
wounds.

## FAILURE

Failure and fear are best friends. They hang out together, just waiting to ruin (and rain on) your life.

What have you bombed at recently?

Unless you understand failure, you will always be scared to try new things. But failure only exists when you believe in it.

What's the worst that can happen? You learn what didn't work. That's it.

You might be scared that your friends will laugh at you, but once you are finished reading this book you will know a thing or two about what is important.

You will make mistakes and fall down and mess up. We all make mistakes, but most people stop following their dreams because they give up.

You have to keep going. You have to keep shining, or the world will get cold and dark and lonely.

The happiest, healthiest, richest people in the world have failed more than anyone else. You better believe it, because that's what it takes to rock!

The more you fail, the closer you are to winning. So let me ask you: what are you going to do the next time things don't work out how you planned?

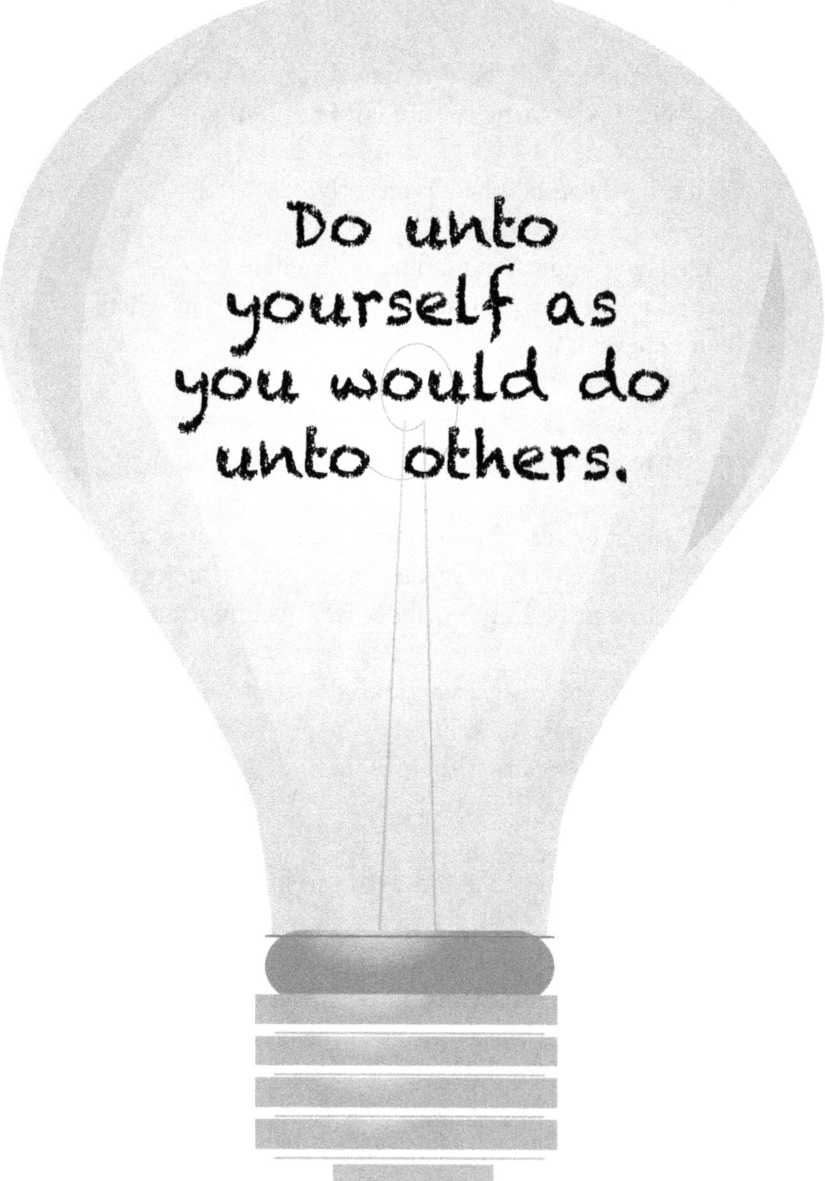

Do unto
yourself as
you would do
unto others.

## ZOMBIES

You might have noticed zombies are loose at your school and they are drooling for a bite of your brain.

Zombies are like sheep. They get together and follow each other around looking for lunch.

All they need to do is take a bite and now you're a zombie too. Run!

Zombies take drugs and skip school and don't care about anything, because they're so busy looking for their next meal.

How do I know so much about zombies?

Because I used to be one. I used to work at a pizza joint called Zombie's Pizza.

I was a dark cloud of despair, undead and loving it.

You probably know that being a zombie is not how you get where you want to go. But what if brains just taste good to you? What then?

Stumbling around in dirty rags without regular showers and proper nutrition will get boring.

So if you haven't been bitten, don't be.

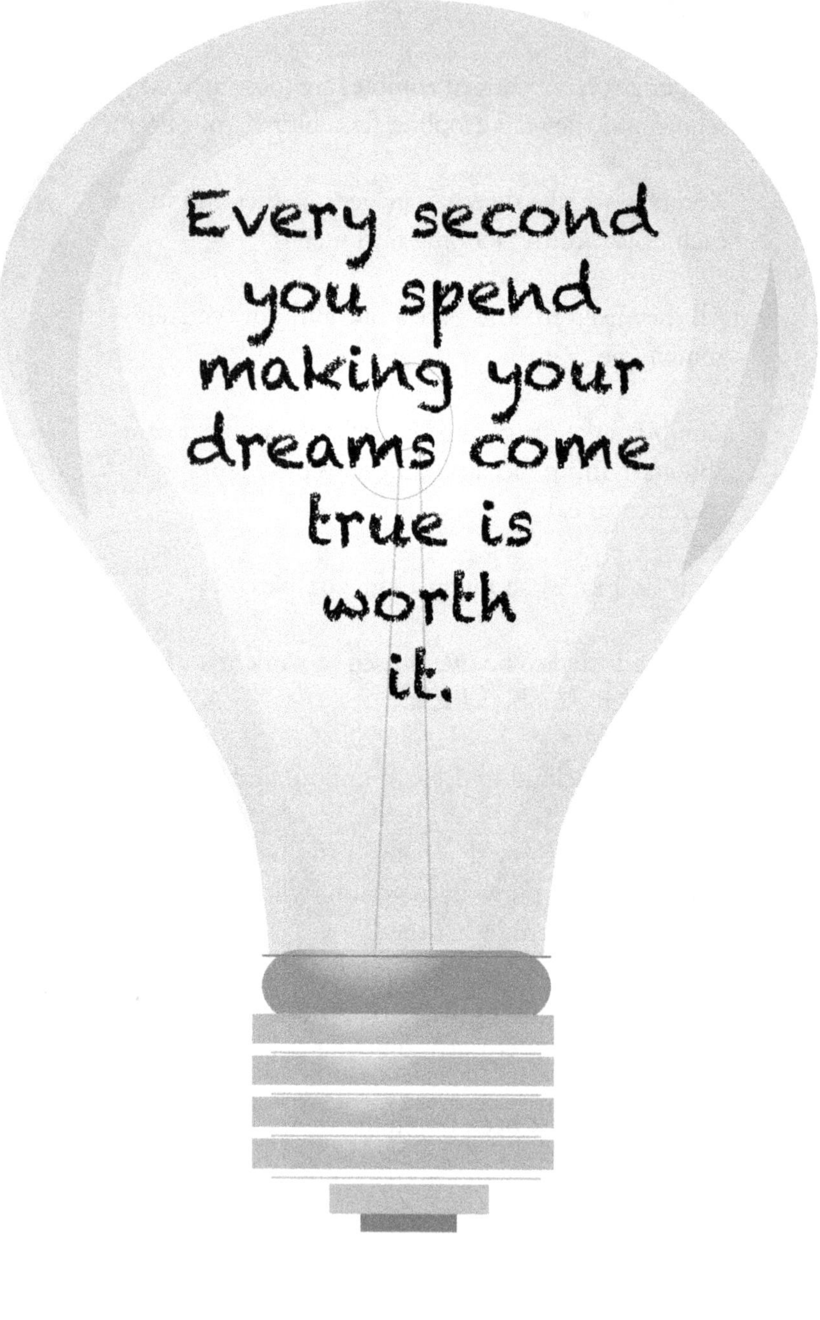

Every second
you spend
making your
dreams come
true is
worth
it.

# HAPPINESS

Bully monsters are not happy people, and there's a reason. They don't spend their time doing what they like, or with people who make them feel happy.

The problem is: they think they do. They think their tribe of gang members are their friends, but they aren't.

Their fellow gang members are lost too, in search of anything to ease the pain they don't know they feel.

Does that make sense?

Sometimes monsters grow up to be adults and STILL don't know what makes them happy. Can you believe that?

The problem is: they get jealous of anyone who knows what they like and has the courage to go after it. They don't like seeing something being done that they fear they can't do themselves (even though they could).

I wish they knew this, but they don't (which is why they rain on your parade). But you know what makes you happy, right?

If you don't know the answer, you better find out (and quick) because love, friends, happiness and fun are all waiting to follow you wherever you go.

Patterns repeat
themselves.
Patterns repeat
themselves.
Patterns...

# PATTERNS

What patterns are you repeating?

You will repeat them over and over again, because even though you shine like the sunshine, you are human.

We all make mistakes, but the happiest people on earth see their mistakes as learning opportunities.

They don't worry about mistakes, so why should you?

Think of all the people and experiences in your life as a reflection, like you're looking into a mirror that's reflecting what you believe deep down inside.

As long as you think / feel / act like life is a certain way, you will see evidence that prove these thoughts / feelings / actions are true.

If you ever want to change your friends, your marks, your job, or your boyfriend or girlfriend, look for patterns and see if you notice when you're about to make the very same choice for the 100th time.

You learned your patterns from your mom and dad, who learned their patterns from their mom and dad.

Asking "why did I do that again?" will either 1) drive you crazy or 2) make you smarter. Choose wisely.

There is no rush. Life is not a race.

## OPPOSITES

There are two sides to every coin (and two sides to every story) as you probably know by now.

Where it gets messy is when the two sides are not clear to everyone involved.

This doesn't mean that opposites aren't there (they are); they just love the game hide-and-seek just like everyone else.

So how do you see them if they aren't always obvious?

You guess.

Maybe you're right and maybe you're wrong, but at least you might see what a bully or frenemy wants or needs deep down.

Bullies only hurt you because they have been hurt too (but don't try to tell them this; people usually don't like to hear the truth about opposites).

We all act in opposite ways all the time. We think one thing, but do the opposite. We say one thing, but do the opposite. We want one thing, but end up chasing after the opposite for some silly reason.

The trick is to know that opposites exist. It will help you understand why we all do the things we do.

Find adults you
trust and ask
for their
help.

## RESPECT

Who do you respect?

Everyone does (even bullies; they probably just forgot and/or are too scared to admit it).

Because we have all been hurt, ignored, laughed at, teased, kicked, punched, spat on, humiliated, hated and disrespected, we get scared of opening up and sharing our own love and respect with the people close to us.

Can you see how this can turn sour pretty quickly? It's kind of like doing the opposite of what we want and then repeating the pattern. Crazy!

Consider this: the sun never says to the earth "you owe me."

How could being like the sun change the world?

See through the disguise of haters, loners and bloodsuckers, because they want love and respect too.

If you can show these evil forces the love and respect they crave deep down, your life will be absolutely amazing (no one does this, by the way).

So why not be the first person on earth to be undeniably AMAZING?!

One day the
bullies will
be gone
forever.

# CREATIVITY

Creativity is like alchemy, the ancient and metaphorical practice of turning lead into gold.

When you turn your dreams into reality, you connect with the source of life and guess what? Shazam!

There is no power on earth like creativity (or the sun).

Creative expression will turn bullies into dust like the sun does to vampires, banishing them forever.

I have seen it happen. My life is proof.

Somehow, your creative forces are like mosquito repellent that make you smell like garlic to vampires, and make you almost invisible to zombies.

How cool is that?

The secret to getting rid of bullies is simple: felt pens or paint or metal or wood or glass or software or tools or musical instruments or paper or fabric or food or film or test tubes or animals. Just start playing and experimenting!

You are a genius, because no one will say it or draw it or sing it or build it or think it or design it or sew it or act it just like you.

So: how will YOU express your feelings and ideas?

Good and bad
come and go.
They always
have and
always will.

## START A BUSINESS

People get paid to make and test video games, design software, help or heal people or animals, design and build buildings, grow food, take us into space, and solve pressing problems.

Some people like to connect people with products and services that improve their lives. Others make beautiful things with their hands, or outrun everyone on their team. Maybe you see solutions to problems not even your teacher can!

If you want to change the world, be your own boss or play by your own rules, you have start your own business or organization.

Why wait until you're older? Why not do it now?

Get your parents to help. If they won't, talk to your favorite relative, or even a teacher you respect.

Yes, you will end up working twice as hard as everyone else, but 1) It's not work when you enjoy it, 2) You have the free time to live your life how you want, and 3) There are no limits to what you can create out of thin air.

Remember: the cream rises to the top!

What will you create / build / sell / do / share?

If it
feels
good
do it.

# VOLUNTEER

A great way to learn new things and meet kids with similar interests is to volunteer for an organization / charity / church / club that is doing work you believe in.

You're looking for your tribe. Give away your time and you will be welcomed into a new family.

Not only will you learn new skills for free, but you may also kickstart a new friendship, hobby or business (which will accelerate your 10,000 hour requirement).

Giving away your time, money and/or energy to others will make you feel good. You may not enjoy instant gratification, but your heart will beat slower, you will worry less, and you may fall in love. Sweet!

Remind yourself that the more you give, the more you get (but not always from where you expect).

Contrary to popular belief, racing through life for fame and fortune will leave you feeling empty, unsatisfied and alone. What good is time, money and energy if you can't share it with other people?

Has the sun ever said "no"?

Keeping all your wonderful gifts and talents and ideas to yourself is not only selfish, it's depressing... Boo!

Are you a wolf
or a sheep?
Pick one.

# DRUGS

Did you know people use drugs to escape reality because they don't know how to deal with their feelings?

When it's metaphorically cloudy all the time, it's easy for people to get depressed and look for happiness by putting toxic substances into their bodies.

They are usually scared or hurt or alone and don't know how to express themselves.

But you can express yourself. You know how. And you know that feelings of fear and failure aren't real (and you know how patterns and opposites work).

Drugs seem harmless at first, but they will keep love and respect out of your life, and probably turn your dreams into nightmares.

What do you know about the long-term side effects?

Drugs are one reason zombies are dead inside and out.

I used to smoke pot to feel cool, but I wasn't (it only made me sick). I thought magic mushrooms would make me marvelous, but they just made me want to run away from everything (and everyone) I loved.

You need all the brain cells you can get, so hang on to them. You will want them later, I guarantee you.

Zombies
have very
special
needs.

## ALCOHOL

If adults could do things in moderation (very few do) then less-than-healthy eating and drinking habits wouldn't be so harmful.

Alcohol causes more problems in the world than you can imagine (which is why I'm asking you to please wait until you are old enough - by law - to try it).

Your brain and body are still growing and the last thing you want is to stunt your growth!

Did you know if you bend a tree when it is young, it will grow up bent?

Do you want to grow up crooked?

Life is way too full of interesting opportunities and adventures to handicap yourself with a learning disability (that you won't be able to detect until it's too late), or put yourself in unneccesary danger.

Alcohol is like poison to your body (and you have enough problems to deal with).

Some people say it's a sad and beautiful world.

I think it's because some things make no sense at all.

At least wait until you are an adult to drink poison.

Define
happiness
for yourself,
because no one
knows it like
you do.

## STRESS

Who stresses you out?
What stresses you out?
When do you get stressed out?
And what do you do when you get stressed out?

There are no right or wrong ways to do anything (as long as you aren't harming anyone or anything) so there are no right or wrong ways to vanquish stress.

If this means running until you can't run anymore, run. If this means dancing until you can't dance anymore, dance. If this means coding until you can't code anymore, code. You get the picture.

For me, baking, drumming, writing and walking are how I clear my head and get rid of stress, anger and frustration.

Sometimes I find the more friends / projects / responsibilities I have, the more fires I have to put out (sometimes it seems like a never-ending battle).

But it's all worth it, because the more fires I put out, the greater the rewards (after the the smoke clears).

The solution is always: find something that you love so much you would do it for free.

Then everything else that seemed to matter so much won't bug you anymore (including bullies).

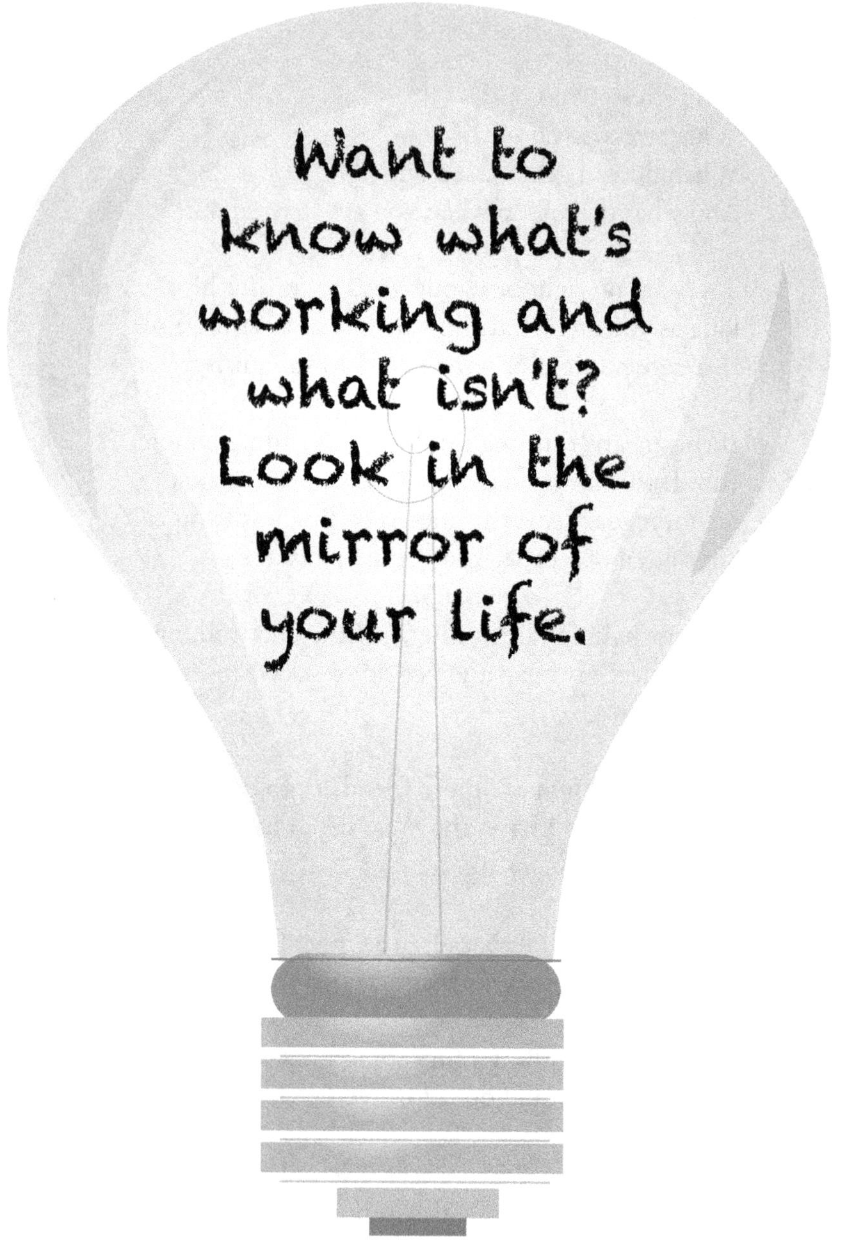

Want to
know what's
working and
what isn't?
Look in the
mirror of
your life.

# GO FOR IT

Your life is going to seem short and long. Some days you will feel like you are going to live forever, yet other days you will feel like you're almost dust.

Even the sun is going to burn out one day, so you don't need anyone's permission to give 'er.

What would inspire you to kick some ass doing what you love?

Even though it may seem like your friends or parents have it all figured out, they don't. No one ever does. All we all do is guess our best guesses, do what needs to be done, and hope for the best. That's it.

This is why you're free to blaze a new trail, take a short cut, see where that goes, and get back on track over and over again... for the rest of your life.

Enjoy the ride, because one day you will be gone, and may wonder why you didn't just go for it!

Imagine you're 80. How will you feel when you remember giving up on something that excited you?

There are seven billion ways to do everything, so do things how you think they should be done.

When people judge you or call you names or say you can't do something, prove them wrong.

Put your life
in good hands.
Your own.

# CRAZY LITTLE ANIMALS

Who in your life acts like a crazy little animal?

Everyone is trying so hard to be 'normal' and civilized and proper and good, but the more you try and be something other than yourself, the more your opposite will come out.

It's nothing to be ashamed of, but trying to hide it just makes it worse. It's like trying to hold a beachball under the water...

1. You're "crazy" because you forget that opposites exist.

2. You're "little" because your inner child is pulling your strings and making you think or feel or do or say one thing, even when you want the opposite.

3. You're an "animal" because humans have lived in caves, hunting and grunting for thousands of years longer than we've lived in boxes and gone shopping at the mall while texting our friends.

When things don't make sense, remember that you're a crazy little animal, like everyone else. It will help.

Keep this fun little morsel of wisdom to yourself, because people often don't like what they don't understand (which is why bullies exist).

So what if your
life is back
to front and
upside
down?

# 10,000 HOURS

I heard it takes about 10,000 hours (or around 10 years) to get really good at something.

The more you practice your musical instrument / dance / compete / study / write essays / make films / show horses, the better you will get.

You've probably noticed how much better you are at a hobby or sport or homework than when you started.

And if you keep at it, one day you'll be a master. Just think of all the possibilities!

You can also squish time.

Instead of spending 10 years to get to 10,000 hours, why not squeeze these 10,000 hours into 5 years?

Wouldn't that be cool? You could do anything.

Once you reach master status, your favorite skill / hobby / sport / talent will become second nature, and your wish will become the world's command.

Why?

Because that's how it works (I've seen it happen over and over and over again.

Don't take my word for it. See it for yourself.

There is only one way to find out if what you believe is true.

## NO RULES

Whose and what rules do you live by?

I know you trust your mom and your dad, and your teachers and everyone else you're supposed to trust.

Following certain rules makes sense (breaking their rules will only stress you out and get you into trouble, as you may know).

When I say there are no rules, I'm talking about the imaginary rules you make up about yourself, your friends and your ideas. If you are not hurting anyone, you are doing nothing wrong.

If there's a voice in your head suggesting you can't do something, you're a crazy little animal (just kidding).

If you think you can't do something, ask yourself: where did that rule come from?

Don't let anyone (even your inner voice) trash-talk your dreams. Not even your best friend. If they do, get rid of them and hang out with other sun-people who dig you.

People who make silly rules about what they (and you) can and can't do, suck. And their lives suck too!

Make rules that give you freedom to be yourself and try new things. Just be safe, take care of the people around you, and have fun!

Learn from
the pros how
to do what
you love.

## MENTORS

Billions of people have lived on the earth and explored every noun in existence. This is both good and bad news for you.

First the bad news: you have to flex your creative muscles a little harder than the zombies around you to come up with something original (which shouldn't be too hard, seeing as you're so smart).

Now the good news: No matter what you're interested in now (and what you become interested in when you grow up) there are people who know a thing or two about it. The best part is: they are everywhere.

More often than not, they will be stoked to talk about what worked and what didn't. Many of them will love helping you get to where you want to go.

Working with mentors who have been-there-done-that has been one of the greatest joys of my life.

I hope you figure it out before I did. It took me forever. I thought I could do it all on my own, but that is impossible (not to mention boring and lonely and expensive).

It doesn't matter how unrealistic other people think your ideas are; there are adults out there you can trust.

Who do you admire and why? They are waiting to help you. What are you going to ask them?

2 steps forward
and 1 step back
will get you
where you
want to
go.

## HIGH SCHOOL

While you are (stuck) in high school, get a head start on your life or business or favorite hobby.

The teachers who listen to you when you talk to them are your allies. You can trust them. Ask them to help you learn what interests you the most.

High school is basic training. It is not enough (unless you are super-motivated AND talented AND have access to resources and movers and shakers to help pave the way).

Regardless, read books and blogs about the things that interest you. Go to conferences if you can.

Spend time away from home and stay away long enough to see things (especially yourself) differently.

When you graduate, remember that student loans are a good investment. Cars aren't. Books are a good investment. Clothes aren't. Lessons are a good investment. Beer isn't.

The more brain cells and creativity and skills you nurture now, the more you will find what you are looking for (love, friendship, health, happiness and money) once you graduate.

What will you do the first year after graduation? What do you need to do to make it happen?

Everything
you see began
with a single
thought.

# THOUGHTS ARE THINGS

If thoughts are things, it makes sense to make sense of things, don't you agree?

The fastest way to make sense of thought-things is by acknowledging that HOW you think of stuff determines HOW the stuff behaves / appears (no matter whether it's a person, place or thing).

Perspective comes in handy when you want to know what nouns are true and which are false.

Knowing this can help you maintain a healthy, balanced, detached perspective on life.

Instead of being fooled by the illusion that something is as it seems, you know that every effect has a cause; is connected; and is worth a closer look.

And you love to learn (especially the important stuff).

Taking responsibility to at least understand the things in your life that make sense (and the things that don't) is one step towards becoming a leader and doing what every awesome person dreams of doing:

Kicking some ass doing what you love.

This is how smart kids navigate their boats to relative calm in the rough storms of the seven seas known as life / school / work / family / relationships.

Your creativity will set you free.

# MINDFULNESS

What is mindfulness?

Mindfulness is knowing that everything is temporary; that nothing lasts.

Mindfulness is knowing that bad marks are a sign (and opportunity) to improve, instead of give up and throw in the towel.

Mindfulness means making your own luck, so when opportunities arise, you can snatch it up and make it all seem easy.

Do you wait around for your friends and classmates to do or say things so you can mentally relax?

If you can't chill, then no grades / honors / scholarships / awards / first prizes will have any effect.

So how do you practice mindfulness?

You can become mindful by meditating; by breathing; by practicing yoga; by walking; by focusing on any activity you enjoy the most.

Doing the things you love to do will put you in a mindful state, and then everything else will just fall into place.

The calmer your mind, the more creative you will be.

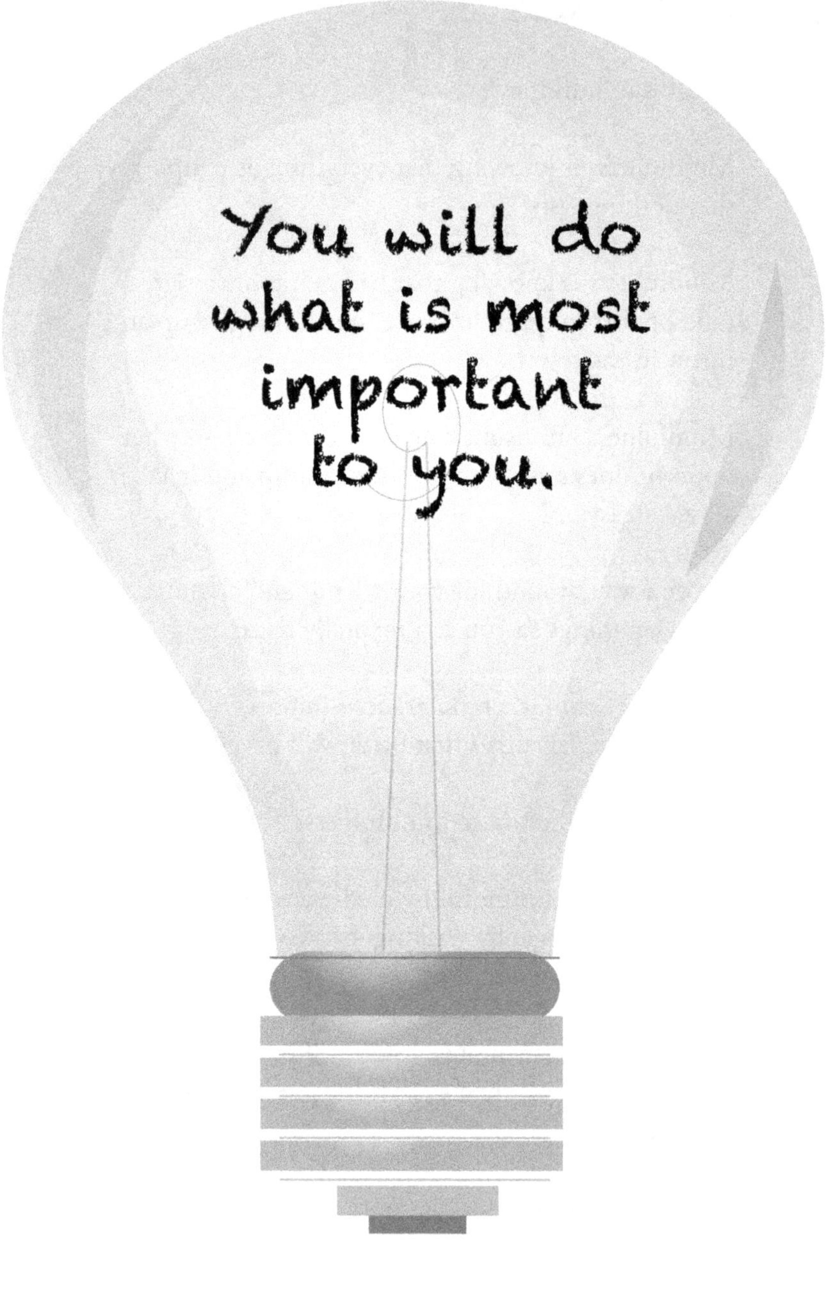

You will do
what is most
important
to you.

# FOOD IS FUEL

If you are what you eat, are you a cookie? Raw broccoli? Egg salad? A cheese burger? Pizza? A stick of celery?

I don't know about you, but they all sound good to me.

Your friends and family probably have some influence over what you eat / when you eat / how you eat / how much you eat.

Are you surrounded with 'healthy' habits?

If you are motivated towards accomplishment, you see doors where others see only walls; doors that lead places you could have never dreamed of.

But those doors will stay locked until you find the skeleton key that opens every door.

How do you get your hands on the skeleton key?

Try eating colorful vegetables, drinking plenty of water, taking it easy on the junk food, eating small portions and chewing your food.

Health is happiness.

Just remember the lyrics to The Hokey-Pokey: That's what it's all about!

You will work
twice as hard
for yourself
but it won't
be work.

# TIME

There seem to be few basic skills more valued than mastering the management of your greatest resource.

I want to arm you with enough silver bullets to slay the insatiable, time-sucking monsters lurking in the shadows hungry to gobble up your time like they were proudly feasting on the all-you-can-eat buffet you call your life.

What would you do with another hour every day?

How would you spend an extra week every year?

It may seem like you're going to live forever, but you won't (you're not a vampire, remember).

So why not make the most of every day?

No matter how you choose to spend your seconds / minutes / hours / days / months / years, the truth is:

If it's important to you, you will make the time.

Remember this when someone says "I don't have time."

This will help you know not only what your own priorities are, but also what other people cherish more than giving you or someone or something else the time it wants or needs.

It is
impossible
to give away
more than
you get.

# WORRY

You may have heard that the only thing to fear is fear itself.

It's a cliché because it's true.

If the only thing to fear is fear itself, then (like fear) the only thing to worry about is worry itself.

But why worry at all? If something is out of your control, there is nothing you can do about it. So why worry about it?

The past is history and the future is a mystery. There is only NOW and there will only ever be NOW.

Worrying about other people, places or things (unfortunate as it is for said nouns) does nothing to help them.

In fact, some people believe that our thoughts have the power / potential to affect those people / places / things (even in far away places).

When you make a mistake (or hear the werewolves howling at your door) simply learn the lesson to be learned, move on, and let worry wither away.

What else are you going to do? Cry yourself to sleep? Lay awake all night tossing and turning? Bite your toenails to the bone? Night time is for sleeping.

No one you
know will be
around when
you are 80.

## PARENTS

Even when it seems like your parents are on the
war path; when they don't seem to get where you're
coming from; when they constantly butt heads
with you; when they get angry over what seems like
nothing; or even when they punish you, they still love
you.

They always will.

But if your parents *really* don't care - as in you do not
feel physically or emotionally safe - please put this
book down now and go and find some adults you can
trust. Believe it or not, there are plenty of grown-ups
who care about kids. Please go and find them.

P.S. This is serious. If you tell the people who decide
things that you are in danger, your life will never be
the same again. Don't cry wolf if one isn't howling.

Okay. Back to the point.

Your parents are likely responsible, supportive, kind
folks who want nothing more than for you to be
happy and healthy and successful.

Give them a break. Sometimes you seem like a little
alien to them!

They don't have all the answers (they never did) and
everyone (everyone) is just making it up as they go.

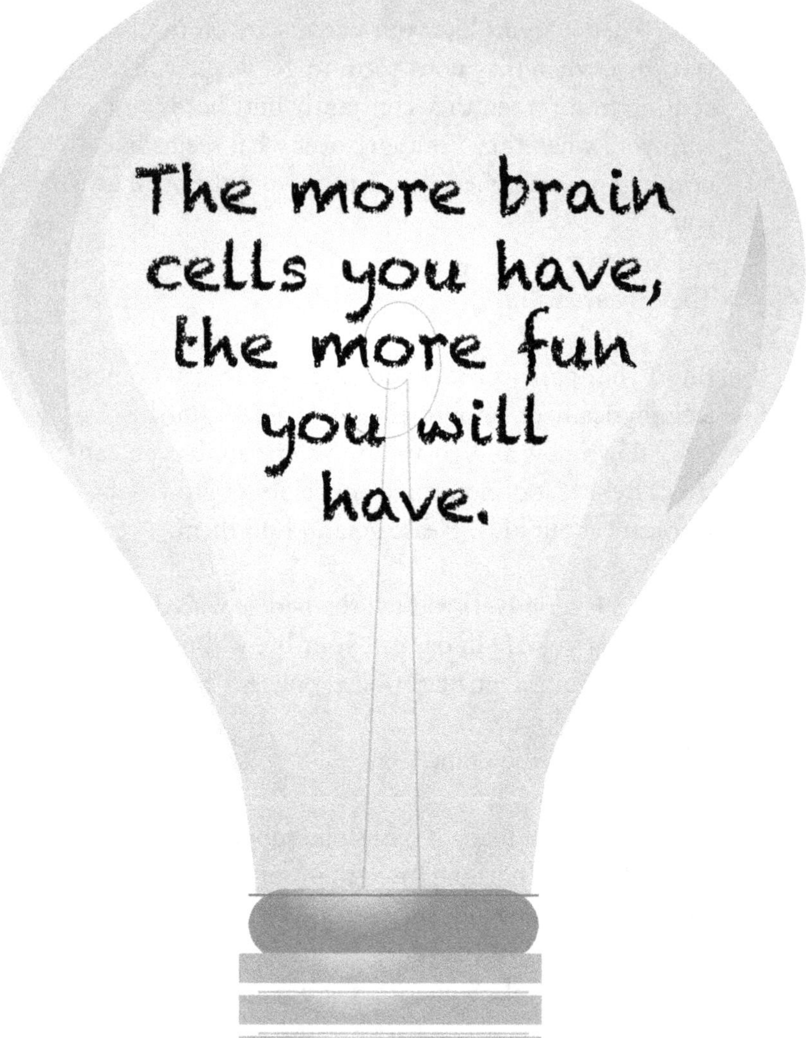

The more brain
cells you have,
the more fun
you will
have.

# FRIENDS

What do you like about your friends?

They probably like the same things you do: the same books; the same movies; the same food; the same clothes.

"Birds of a feather flock together" is a neat rhyme I like. That's what makes friendship so cool; sharing common interests, values, likes and dislikes makes everything in life seem easier.

But just because you have a lot of friends on social media doesn't mean they are your true friends.

In a battle between quality versus quantity, quality is always the winner (unless you really don't care about people, in which case you probably aren't reading this book).

Why? Because friends are the best thing on earth!

Your friends are your friends because they make you feel good (if they don't, you better get some new ones).

Hopefully you aren't taking on water... because you the old joke says:

What's the only type of boat you can't easily sink?

A Friend Ship.

Find ways to
get naturally
high instead.

# SPIRITUALITY

The only advice I can give you about spirituality is to believe what you want and find your own way.

Yes, your parents wield a little influence; they will teach you (both consciously and unconsciously) what they believe, though when you start thinking for yourself, know that it's okay to make up your own mind if and when you feel like you want to.

There is no one right or wrong way.

If you don't believe me, take a look around. This is one of the only reasons people fight.

People fight because they think other people are crazy to believe in something other than what they are supposed to believe in.

It's that simple (and ironic, because you would think 'spiritual' people would be able to practice unconditional love, patience and compassion.

The problem may be religion, because my definition of spirituality how you understand your connection to whomever or whatever gave you the breath of life and makes the grass grow with seemingly zero effort.

The point is: you can listen to what other people say, or you can decide what YOU believe. It's up to you.

Question
anyone who
says that
something
is wrong.

# EVERYTHING IS TEMPORARY

Your friends may not always be your friends and your family won't be around forever.

You will change jobs and live in different houses. You may even call different cities (or countries) home.

You may get married and you may get divorced.

Every single relationship you ever have will shift and change and grow and decay in its own way, according to its own timetable.

You can't control or hinder or block anyone or anything from making their own decisions or choosing what is right (and when) for them.

Doing the opposite will drive you insane.

Throughout your life your heart will break over and over again. But your ability to love will grow stronger and stronger. The secret is to ensure the latter happens more than the former.

If you remember that everything is temporary, your life will be a lot easier, I promise.

Remember this, and you won't be so surprised and shocked when something changes.

Because it will.

Work for
free and you
will see.

## TRAVEL

One of the wisest words ever spoken about travel
came out of Saint Augustine's mouth.

He said: The world is a book. Those who don't travel
read only a page.

Forget the 7 Wonders of the World; have you been to
another country? Or across the ocean?

Most people are scared to leave their home town,
state, province, region or country. But what they are
most scared of is facing the unknown.

They fear unfamiliar food, language, customs, clothes,
rules, ideas, trends, and getting lost or feeling lonely.

But no school or training or program or sport or
hobby will give you the same education as traveling
(or living) in another country (even for just a few
months).

Do whatever you can to get away from home when
you graduate (even just for a summer).

You won't regret it.

Traveling alone (or with a friend) will change your life
more than you can imagine; the wonders that await
you in distant lands will blow your mind (in a good
way).

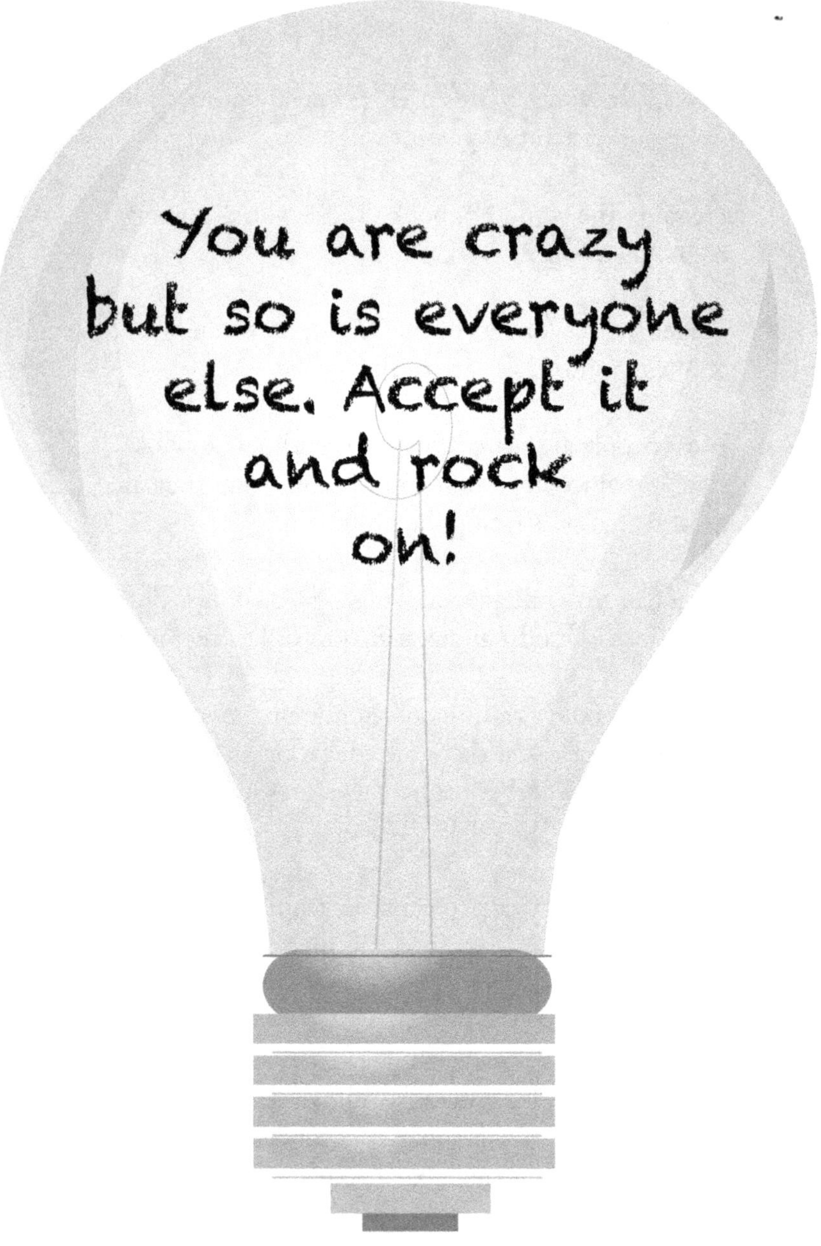

You are crazy
but so is everyone
else. Accept it
and rock
on!

# POPULARITY

Ideally, you are always in the right place at the right time, right?

Ideally, you regularly step out of your comfort zone and take social risks (instead watching from the sidelines and waiting for someone else to make you rich, famous, popular, intelligent and successful).

What makes people popular? Self confidence.

How do you get self confidence?

Do the things you like to do (including learning what matters to you) and forget about everything else.

Forget the bullies and focus on doing your best.

If you see an opportunity to volunteer for a social or political event that excites you, dive right in. Join the clubs and associations focused on creating / developing / promoting / funding / celebrating and working towards goals that are important to you.

People focused on achieving their goals will be your best friends; your relationships will strengthen over time and bring you rewards for decades to come.

Making friends is easy when you are being true to yourself. Speak from your heart and you will attract the best friends and soul mates on earth.

Remembering where you came from will remind you who you are.

## MONEY

Just like zombies are addicted to brains, most adults are addicted to money. They think it will bring them love, happiness and respect (so they get hooked).

But it can't buy love; it can't buy happiness; and it doesn't buy respect. So if it can't give you the things you want, what's it good for?

Money makes it easier to acquire the goods and services you desire. That's it.

People get high on money (distracted) chasing bigger and better stuff (and more of it) to help them ignore the fact they don't have the love, happiness or respect they want.

But they seem to be hallucinating, because the best things in life aren't things. In fact, they cost zilch::

- Laughter
- Love
- Peace
- Time
- Family
- Friendship

Until you can be happy with nothing, you will never be happy with anything.

Make money work for you, not the other way around.

The smartest,
friendliest
people are also
the coolest.
You'll see.

# FINANCIAL FREEDOM

You are lucky.

If you heed the following advice, you will be better off than the majority of people in the world.

Plus, you can either retire long before anyone else (or with more money, to help you buy things you don't need to please people you don't like).

If you have a part-time job, save a bit of money every day and ask your parents to help you invest it.

Do your own research and teach yourself what you need to know so you can ask intelligent questions.

If your parents will help you, great! If not, ask them to make an appointment at the bank and drop you off.

Google: "compound interest" and see for yourself what you can make possible by starting a simple, steady and slow investing strategy for yourself.

This will eventually guarantee (as much as is possible) your future financial freedom, so you won't have to work at a job you don't like for the rest of your life.

Investing your money will make you a dragon-slayer.

P.S. Few teenagers do this. If you want to be a millionaire one day, do this (you're welcome).

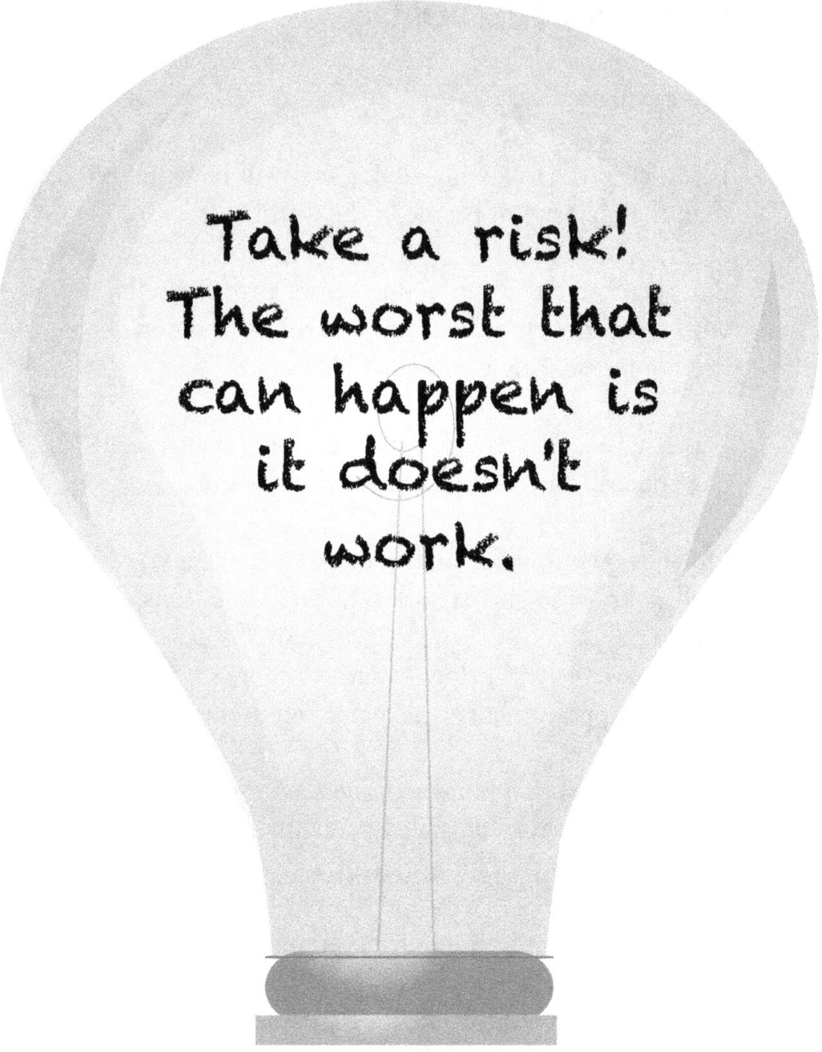

Take a risk!
The worst that
can happen is
it doesn't
work.

# RADICAL ACCEPTANCE

Radical acceptance is unusual because few people accept themselves and their circumstances as they are.

But if you can deal with your problems with the attitude that "this too shall pass" then you may just have found the answer to a long and happy life.

So: what are you going to do the next time you can't change something?

What will you say to all those mayhem-making monsters that will inevitably come marauding through your peaceful meadow or enchanted forest looking to do some serious damage?

Like fear and worry, the only other boobie trap you would do well to avoid is 'sweating the small stuff'.

If you can let nouns go (they eventually go their own way on their own schedule anyway) you may well enjoy another secret to life foreign to so many people.

What else are you going to do? Bang your head against a brick wall? Go crazy? Run away?

Vampires are not worth the blood loss, zombies will always be zombies, and princesses will never be satisfied (same goes for people in the real world).

Accept them for who they are and move on.

Eat less or exercise more and your body will love you.

## EXERCISE

Once you find and follow your bliss (and figure out how to forgive the big bad bullies) exercising will get you where you want to go even faster.

For example: if you love pizza, why not eat it once a week (instead of every day) and burn it off with your favorite physical activity, so you can live longer and eat even more pizza?

Who knows what innovative pizza recipes / flavors / designs / delivery options will be around when you're 80. Aren't you curious to see the future?

Enjoy your lightning-fast metabolism while you can, because once you turn 30, your metabolism will slow down a bit and will stop burning calories on autopilot.

It's easy: walk or ride your bike instead of taking the bus or driving. Go swimming or jogging or hiking.

Just like financial gurus advise earning more than you spend (or spending less than you earn) simply burn more calories than you eat (or eat fewer calories than you burn).

If you could just crawl into a jam-filled donut or sip soda all day, earn it with exercise (before or after you indulge in the finest of sugary snacks).

The healthier you are, the happier you will be.

Find someone
you admire and
ask them for
help. They will
love it.

## BABY STEPS

Hit songs, blockbuster movies, gold medals and lifetime achievement awards are impressive (and possibly intimidating) though every rockstar, producer and athelete started from scratch.

Some people have natural talent, wealthy parents, or an older brother or sister to look out for them, but so what if you don't?

The harder you have to work for something, the more it will mean to you. I mean it.

Instead of being overwhelmed by the fame, fortune, fun and the fabulous lifestyles of the people in your life and on TV, remember they started where you did.

What does the first step toward your goal look like?

First, see the end result in your imagination. Now work backwards and divide each step into smaller steps, until each step seems possible. Once you know the steps, you take one at a time until you get there.

You can always edit your book, draw another picture, go back to school, try out for the team next year, study harder for the next exam, or redo anything.

You can always correct what other people call mistakes, because if you love something, you will always get better at it. That's what successful people do.

When it comes
to innovation
make your
own rules.

## YOUR PURPOSE

What were you born to do?

P.S. No one knows the answer to this one but you.

Nobody.

That's why it's YOUR purpose.

You may have noticed by now that this book is all about finding and following your bliss so you can squash the blood-suckers swarming around you who maybe make life more difficult than you would like it to be.

Figuring out what you love to do more than anything is the most important - albeit - perhaps the only real purpose (ha!) to life.

Without passion for your personal mission, your life may always be devoid of deep meaning. That sucks.

This is what leads people to commit suicide and do drugs and hang out with vampires and zombies and turn into brain-devouring cannibals or even worse: find themselves undead for eternity relying on the living for their survival.

I don't know about you, but as romantic as that may be for the first few weeks, I bet the shine starts to fade as soon as the novelty wears off.

Hurt people
hurt people.
It's just what
they do.

## ROTTEN APPLES

It's unfortunate, but some apples rot on the tree (if they even grow into formed fruit at all).

Either they don't get enough water or sunlight or fertilizer. Or maybe the tree is very old and tired.

Whatever the reason, even the 'deformed' apples are a natural part of life (because nature gave them life).

By apples I'm talking about other people.

Maybe some kids at school are rotten apples; maybe even some adults you know seem extra crabby!

You may not like some teachers, but they aren't rotten apples; your relationship with them (a 2-way street, btw) is what's rotten. But that's another book. Or is it?

I have found we all have 2 choices in the matter:

1. Accept the fact rotten apples will always exist.
2. Get frustrated and angry, etc.

If you choose #1, you can either help them (a friendly and compassionate approach) or simply leave them alone (don't bully or provoke them).

#2 will leave you miserable (and perhaps no better than the bullies you wish to banish). You always have a choice, in every situation, no matter what.

The more you
learn the more
you earn.

# COLLEGE

You are going to love college. It's a blast!

It will seem like a whole other world, and high school will seem light years away.

College is a chance to start over, find your tribe, and have a lot of fun (while gaining invaluable skills in business, a trade, or your chosen career).

Some of the friends you make at college will be your friends forever. Sweet!

You may meet the man or woman of your dreams (it happens all the time) while exploring nearly any field of study or activity or creative profession you desire.

You can dip your toes into any interest (and enjoy the guidance, support and resources of entire industries, professionals and experts ready and willing to help).

Student loans are one of the best investments you can make. Higher education will enable you to earn more money over the course of the next 50-plus years.

P.S. But why retire when you love what you do?

Better jobs, careers and business ventures pay off better than crappy, minimum-wage gigs every day of the week. Remember: the more you learn, the more you earn.

Love is
like a butterfly.
Chase it and
it flies away.

# LOVE

Love is like a butterfly. If you chase it, it flies away. But if you follow your bliss, it will find you.

And you will always know if it's true once he or she does come and find you on the other side of the world (or in cyberspace), for time is to love what wind is to fire; it extinguishes the small and kindles the great.

These 2 morsels of wisdom have kept my heart warm while (in some ways) my life has seemed out of my control (if you don't believe me, take a look around and see how little control you have over other people and circumstances).

But you also can't control your heart. It will love who and when it wants. You may have no say!

Whether you have been in love or not; whether you've been on a date or not; whether you have a boyfriend or girlfriend or not; and whether you have your eye on someone (or not) doesn't change the fact that you want to give and receive love.

Be patient. It will happen. Remember the butterfly

Also remember that couples who stay together for 60 years go through ups and downs. There are no rules (except the ones you make up together).

Enjoy the game of love like you enjoy the game of life.

You are
loved.

# TRUST YOURSELF

No one knows the future, so make it yours.

And no one knows you like you do, so don't be afraid to change things up as you go along.

You can reinvent yourself daily (new surroundings such as other countries and cultures help a lot).

You can overcome most challenges as long as you don't give up. But if you think you can't, you're probably right.

If you want something, don't wait for other people to give you permission or say YES or OK or GO.

Too many people follow everyone else around like sheep, while vampires prey on their souls, suck the life out of them, and leave them cursed like they are, shivering in the shadows cast by their clouds.

But not you. You are the sun.

And the sun is always shining, even when it's behind the clouds.

The sun is loved by everyone and everything on earth.

And so are you.

Good luck, bully-cloud-banisher!

## THE INSPIRATION FOR THIS BOOK

Before I was born, my uncle Phil wrote me a letter and began it with *Dear Leroy* (my mum still won't give it to me).

Years later, after dropping out of high school due to extreme bullying, my cousin Bonnie lent me her guitar. Over the next year I learned how to express myself with words and music, and eventually write and record simple songs.

Through this process I empowered myself with what I call *Creative Confidence,* because when I returned to school I was bully-proof.

Problem solved.

The most valuable lesson I learned on my journey from vampire victim to vampire slayer was the courage to take creative risks, learn from the people I trusted, seek the truth (what made the most sense to me) and kick some ass doing what I love.

This book was written to help you express your unique creativity, connect with the people you dig, and celebrate your life in your own special way, so you can *forgive the bully and follow your bliss.*

I wish you all the creativity, adventure, warmth and wealth in the world.

Oliver Luke Delorie
Gabriola Island, British Columbia
July 5th, 2017

9 780099 484686